Geology

Rachel L. McDonald

Geology, Technology and Human Behaviour

Fatal Accidents in Scottish Coal Mines

LAP LAMBERT Academic Publishing

Impressum / Imprint
Bibliografische Information der Deutschen Nationalbibliothek: Die Deutsche Nationalbibliothek verzeichnet diese Publikation in der Deutschen Nationalbibliografie; detaillierte bibliografische Daten sind im Internet über http://dnb.d-nb.de abrufbar.
Alle in diesem Buch genannten Marken und Produktnamen unterliegen warenzeichen-, marken- oder patentrechtlichem Schutz bzw. sind Warenzeichen oder eingetragene Warenzeichen der jeweiligen Inhaber. Die Wiedergabe von Marken, Produktnamen, Gebrauchsnamen, Handelsnamen, Warenbezeichnungen u.s.w. in diesem Werk berechtigt auch ohne besondere Kennzeichnung nicht zu der Annahme, dass solche Namen im Sinne der Warenzeichen- und Markenschutzgesetzgebung als frei zu betrachten wären und daher von jedermann benutzt werden dürften.

Bibliographic information published by the Deutsche Nationalbibliothek: The Deutsche Nationalbibliothek lists this publication in the Deutsche Nationalbibliografie; detailed bibliographic data are available in the Internet at http://dnb.d-nb.de.
Any brand names and product names mentioned in this book are subject to trademark, brand or patent protection and are trademarks or registered trademarks of their respective holders. The use of brand names, product names, common names, trade names, product descriptions etc. even without a particular marking in this work is in no way to be construed to mean that such names may be regarded as unrestricted in respect of trademark and brand protection legislation and could thus be used by anyone.

Coverbild / Cover image: www.ingimage.com

Verlag / Publisher:
LAP LAMBERT Academic Publishing
ist ein Imprint der / is a trademark of
OmniScriptum GmbH & Co. KG
Bahnhofstraße 28, 66111 Saarbrücken, Deutschland / Germany
Email: info@lap-publishing.com

Herstellung: siehe letzte Seite /
Printed at: see last page
ISBN: 978-3-659-81299-6

Zugl. / Approved by: Stirling, The University of Stirling, Dissertation 2015

Copyright © 2015 OmniScriptum GmbH & Co. KG
Alle Rechte vorbehalten. / All rights reserved. Saarbrücken 2015

Contents

		Page
Acknowledgments		2
Chapter One	Introduction	3
Chapter Two	Fixed Working Conditions	17
Chapter Three	Technology	34
Chapter Four	Human Behaviour	55
Chapter Five	Conclusion	71
Bibliography		75

Acknowledgments

The Stirling University History department have been a constant support throughout my time at University, and have helped me develop an even deeper interest in the subject. I would especially like to thank my Supervisor, Catherine Mills, for all of her help, support and patience. Her guidance has been invaluable, and without which this research would have been far harder.

To all of my friends and family who have always been supportive, and on hand for assistance; in particular to my parents, without them, this research, and in fact the last four years, would not have been possible.

To the Stirling University Equestrian Club for all of their sympathy, advice and for always being there to cheer me up when I needed it most. You have made this research and my time at Stirling far more enjoyable.

Chapter One: The Coal Mining Industry

"The most painful feature of the coalmining industry is the heavy toll it takes on human life by accidents causing death and injury"[1]

Coal mining in the 19th century was hard work and conditions were appalling. Miners often worked in confined spaces deep below the ground that were wet, noisy, dusty and poorly illuminated. Labour was hazardous. Miners were surrounded by numerous dangers. There was always the chance that a roof above could cave in if not properly supported, unstable rocks falling from above was another such danger. Ladders, gunpowder blasting and machinery all potentially posed risks. A significant hazard, especially in the mid-19th Century, was the presence of naturally occurring gases such as methane (firedamp) and carbon dioxide (chokedamp). These could suffocate a miner if the underground workings were not properly ventilated or they could be ignited if improper safety lamps, candles or any naked flames were used.[2] An example of an incident involving an explosion of methane occurred at Blantyre Number 1 Pit on July 2nd 1879. 28 men were killed as a result.[3] In his report, the District Mines Inspector stated that all those who could have given evidence as to the origin of the explosion were killed and it could only be assumed that there was a naked light present, which must have been lit by a workman.[4] Therefore, hazards

---

[1] Bulman H.F., *Coal Mining and the Coal Miner* (London, 1920) p 61
[2] Methane is a colourless gas, normally odourless as well; it is found near the roof of a mine and is extremely flammable. A build up of carbon dioxide in the underground environment creates an atmosphere that is unable to sustain normal respiration.
[3] Annual Reports of the Mines Inspectors, *Parliamentary Papers,* (1879) p 244
[4] Annual Reports of the Mines Inspectors, *Parliamentary Papers,* (1879) p 244

created by other workers were a factor to consider when looking at unsafe working conditions. Notwithstanding accident hazards, a miner's health could still be seriously damaged by their work. For example, dust damaged miner's lungs, repetitive movements in confined spaces resulted in musculoskeletal disorders and poor illumination damaged their sight.[5] Although there is a great deal of information on miners' health, this study will focus solely on accidents due to space constraints.

There was very little occupational mortality data collected prior to 1850. Hair's study on mortality rates in British Coal Mines from 1800-1850 is where the best estimates on accident mortality can be found. He makes it clear that the mortality rate in British Coal mines was around 5 deaths per thousand men per annum from 1800 to 1850.[6] This compares unfavourably to agricultural labourers. A collier roughly lived until he was 36 years old, whilst an agricultural labourer lived for 62 years.[7]

At the beginning of the 19th century men, women and children were all working underground in these conditions. This was exposed by the 1842 Royal Commission on the Employment of Women and Children in Mines, which was an investigation into the condition of female and child labour. Its publication caused

---

[5] McIvor, A & Johnston, R., *Miners' lungs: a history of dust disease in British coal mining* (Aldershot, 2007) & Mills, C. *Regulating Health and Safety in the British Mining Industries, 1800-1914* (Surry, 2010)

[6] Hair, P.E.H. Mortality from Violence in British Coal Mines, 1800-50, *Economic History Review,* Vol. 21 Issue 3 (December 1968) pp 545-561

[7] Mills, C. *Regulating Health and Safety in the British Mining Industries, 1800-1914* (Surry, 2010) pp 1-2

widespread dismay at how awful the conditions were for all underground labour.[8] The report made clear that it was common for children as young as eight, and sometimes even younger to be employed at tasks beyond their responsibility and understanding. Such as ventilation, which increased the risk of fatal injury. Any error of judgement or dereliction of duty could result in a build up of methane and subsequent explosion. To ensure its message to Members of Parliament was enforced the Commission included graphic images of the women and children at work.[9]

Before the mid-19th century, mines were not regulated by health and safety laws. Legislation began in 1842, following the Royal Commission, with the Mines and Collieries Act. It was hastily passed, and was not about the promotion of mining safety as such, but about reform of the abuses connected with the employment of women and children underground.[10] Although it did not contain any safety provision, it did have an indirect impact on the risk of accidents, as children were no longer employed in positions of responsibility such as being in charge of ventilation and haulage. In 1850 the Coal Mines Inspection Act was passed, this was the first act that dealt directly with major safety issues. It was a temporary measure only. Under the legislation four Mines Inspectors were appointed and the British coalfield was divided into four inspection districts. The Act also gave the inspectors the power to collect information about fatal accidents in mines in their district. The Coal Mines

---

[8] Royal Commission on the Employment of Women and Children in mines, *Parliamentary Papers,* 1942, p 128
[9] Royal Commission on the Employment of Women and Children in mines, *Parliamentary Papers,* 1942, p 120
[10] Sinclair, J. *Coal Mining Law,* (London, 1958) p 81

Inspection Act of 1855 made the 1850 Act permanent and decided that the Country should be split into 12 districts with 12 Mines Inspectors. In 1862 it became compulsory to provide each mine with two exits and the minimum age limit for working in mines was raised from ten to twelve years. The 1872 Coal Mines Act brought the laws together and expanded on safety legislation. For example, every colliery had to be managed by a person holding a certificate of competency obtained by state examination, and mine workers now had the right to appoint their own representatives to inspect mines and raise safety concerns with the inspectorate.[11] The working day for boys underground was reduced to ten hours and they were also required to attend school for 20 hours in a fortnight. The 1872 Act essentially laid down the foundations for current legislation.

The 12 districts allowed the Country to be split into manageable geographical areas that could be more closely monitored by inspectors. These inspectors ensured that a set of 'General Rules' were implemented. These were regulations that applied to all collieries, so they were not specific to local conditions such as differences in rock type or the presence of gases. For example the Fife coalfield was notoriously gassy, whilst the Lanarkshire pits were more prone to unstable bedrock.[12] Inspectors also had the power to implement 'Special Rules'; these dealt with the local

---

[11] Sinclair, J. *Coal Mining Law,* (London, 1958) p 85
[12] Chuch, R. *The History of the British Coal Mining Industry Vol.3: 1830-1913 Victorian Pre-eminence* (Oxford, 1986) p 150

differences and were subordinate to the General Rules.[13] Therefore in theory all mines should have been on a level playing field in terms of safety. An example of a Special Rule implemented by William Alexander, Inspector of Coal Mines for the Western District of Scotland in 1856 was '[I]f from accident or other cause, colliers are at any time unable to find a sufficient supply of prop wood at the pithead, when it is unsafe to continue their work without it, they are expressly forbidden to remain at their working places.'[14] If Special Rules were not followed fines could be levied by the mining company, whereas a breach of General Rules resulted in a court case.

Despite the level playing field in regulatory controls rates of accident mortality differed between inspection districts. For example if the mortality rate for the East and West of Scotland is examined, there are marked differences. See graphs 1:1 and 1:2 below.

---

[13] Chuch, R. *The History of the British Coal Mining Industry Vol.3: 1830-1913 Victorian Pre-eminence* (Oxford, 1986) p 148
[14] Scottish Mining Website, 'Colliery Rules' (2005), < http://www.scottishmining.co.uk/13.html> [Accessed 24.10.2014]

Graph 1:1

Mortality Rate Per 1000 Men (East)

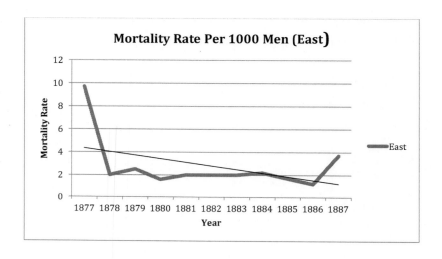

Graph 1:2

Mortality Rate Per 1000 Men (Western District)

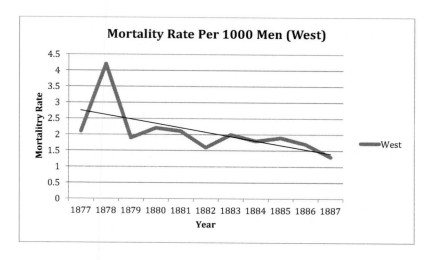

Although legislation had been repeatedly strengthened and in operation for some 27 years despite there being a downward trend, there are still a great number of deaths occurring per year. Coal mining was still a dangerous occupation. The two graphs however raise the question why were accident mortality rates in each district so different when they were all legislated by the same law?

This study will focus on and compare the East and the West of Scotland inspection districts. The fact that Scotland is only split into two districts means that a direct national comparison can be undertaken. The Mining Inspectorate collected a significant amount of qualitative and quantitative data, which was published annually in their reports. Accidents were categorised by cause (18 categories in total) and the age of the fatally injured. These Reports provide the main primary source for the study. The statistical evidence provides the foundations for analysis, which gives this study its grounding and they have been converted into detailed graphs, which opens a window onto safety in each district. This study focuses on the period from 1877-1887. This period has been selected because it gives the 1872 act, which was based upon 22 years of regulation, time to be effective and essentially 'bed in'.

There is a vast amount of literature on coal mining, to the extent that there are published bibliographies, for example Benson and Neville's *Bibliography of the British Coal Industry*.[15] The literature can be categorised into three main sections, social, economic, and technological histories. This brief literature review will provide

---

[15] Benson, J & Neville, R. *Bibliography of the British Coal Industry,* (Oxford, 1981)

a discussion of a sample of the key texts relevant to this study. In terms of general histories *A short History of the Coal Mining Industry,* produced by the Scottish division of the National Coal Board in 1958, gives the reader an overview of the mining industry as a whole, as well as making clear the numerous hazards that miners faced, such as gases, rock falls and dust.[16] As it was produced by the National Coal Board, there is always the possibility that there is bias present. However, overall this volume is effective in giving the reader an insight into accident risks that the miners faced and begins to direct further reading into the types of hazards present. Published in 1986, Church et al's *The History of the British Coal Mining Industry Vol.3 1830- 1913,* is an extensive volume that covers all aspects of the British coal mining industry. Church dedicates a significant amount of space to regulation, which allows the reader to gain a deeper insight into the provision of safety measures and in turn develop a greater understanding of how the law operated.[17] Duncan's 2005 publication *The Mine Workers,* has insightful sections written from a miner's perspective, including legislation and accidents. It offers first hand accounts of the conditions miners worked in, making clear how cramped and dark the collieries were.[18] It also discusses the miner's use of the safety lamp and the role of naked flames and gas.[19] This highlights questions about technology in relation to safety and human behaviour. *British Coal Miners in the Nineteenth Century,* written by John

---

[16] McGregor, M. *A Short History of the Scottish Coal Mining Industry* (1958)

[17] Chuch, R. *The History of the British Coal Mining Industry Vol.3: 1830-1913 Victorian Pre-eminence* (Oxford, 1986)

[18] Duncan, R. *The Mine Workers* (Edinburgh, 2005) p 150

[19] Duncan, R. *The Mine Workers* (Edinburgh, 2005) p 153

Benson discusses the social aspects of the industry in the nineteenth century.[20] Benson again emphasises poor working conditions.

In 1924, the Mining Association of Great Britain published a volume that covered all aspects of the British coal mining industry.[21] The Mining Association was what would become the National Union of Mineworkers in 1945. The volume devotes a detailed chapter to accidents, which is categorised by cause. The text makes it clear there were more explosions of gas in the East than in the West of Scotland but does not discuss this in any detail.

In terms of accidents more specifically, Wyman's in his study of Americans miners and the industrial revolution, takes the stance that the introduction of new technology created new hazards for miners to navigate.[22] Technology is a key aspect of this study and so Wyman's stance is useful as a comparison with the British miners' testimony on safety lamps researched by Duncan as discussed above. *A History of Coal Mining in Great Britain,* discusses the advancement of scientific and technological knowledge.[23] The hazards associated with lighting and ventilation are looked at in depth, making clear that they caused difficulties when it came to safe working practices. The entire book concerns mines safety and contains a great deal of information concerning technology, such as improvements in haulage techniques, in

---

[20] Benson, J. *British Coal Miners in the Nineteenth Century* (London, 1980)

[21] The Mining Association of Great Britain, *The Historical Review of Coal Mining,* (London, 1924)

[22] Wyman, M. *Hard Rock Epic: Western Miners and the Industrial Revolution, 1860-1910*, (California, 1992) pp 16-17

[23] Galloway, R.L., *A history of coal mining in Great Britain* (London, 1969)

mines, which is of great importance to this study. It raises the question, does technology make a mine safer or does it introduce new risks as Wyman argues? What was the role of technology in the two Scottish districts? Can technology advance explain either the higher rate of accidents in the East district or does it account for the lower rate in the West?

Published in 2000, Brown's study of Western American coal mining suggests that 'big' coal mining companies were safer than smaller individually run collieries.[24] Likewise how will this assertion compare to Scotland? Again can company size account for the higher rate of accidents in the East district?

In terms of legislation, Boyd's *Coal Mines Inspection, Its History and Results*, published in 1879, *gives* a narrative of the early days of coal mining regulation.[25] Which allows the reader an insight into the conditions in early 19th Century coalmines, pre legislation. Sir Andrew Bryan's *The Evolution of Health and Safety in Mines* makes clear the dangers of coal mining and discusses the regulation of the industry, with reference to the difference regulation made to accident rates.[26] However it should be noted that Bryan was Chief Inspector of Mines from 1947-51, and may have wanted to paint a picture of progress, so there may be some exaggeration of improvements. Despite this it gives the reader an insight into whether the law had an impact on accident rates. Following on from this, Sinclair's *Coal*

---

[24] Brown, R. *Hard Rock Miners: The intermountain West, 1860-1920,*(Texas, 2000) p 81
[25] Boyd, N. *Coal Mines Inspection, Its History and Results* (London, 1879)
[26] Bryan, A. *The Evolution of Health and Safety in Mines* (1975)

Mining Law, provides a great deal of information on legislation from the beginning of the 19th century to 1954.[27] It covers all the acts throughout this period in great detail and provides an excellent background to all aspects of legislation.

Mills's 2010, *Regulating Health and Safety in the British Mining Industries 1800-1914,* gives a comprehensive overview of health and safety in all of Britain's mining industries.[28] The sections on mining legislation are especially useful to the reader. The section about metal mines is specifically helpful as the miners in this sector of the industry work in hard rock, which is stable and less prone to falls and explosive gas is uncommon. This implies that the geology of a mine may influence the accident rate. It also gives information on the idea of there being a collective accident risk in coal that isn't present in metal mining. The idea of collective risk is based on the fact that one man's action could kill many; so one man smoking could cause a gas explosion that kills many of his colleagues. This directs the reader's attention to elements of human error when considering reasons for accidents in coalmines. Mills's in *Does Familiarity Breed Contempt* article discusses accident behaviour, and makes clear why some miners were more likely to take risks than others and in turn cause accidents.[29] This is useful to the study due to its discussion on accident behaviour in terms of age and argues that the experienced middle-aged miners became complacent and more likely to take risks. This is echoed in the Mines

---

[27] Sinclair, J. *Coal mining Law* (London, 1958)

[28] Mills, C. *Regulating Health and Safety in the British Mining Industries, 1800-1914* (Surry, 2010)

[29] Mills, C. 'Does Familiarity Breed Contempt?' Age and Accident Frequency in Cornish Non-Ferrous Metal Mining, 1881-1901' *British Mining,* No. 75 (2004)

Inspectors Reports, for example Mr Moore, the Mines Inspector for the Eastern district of Scotland; in 1872 suggested accidents were down to a miner's negligence.[30] Is age as well as careless behaviour implicated in the differing rates of accident mortality for Scotland?

Some studies focus on the nature of hazards such as Helen and Baron Duckham's *Great Pit Disasters,* published in 1973. It gives an explanation of the dangers that have affected the British mining industry.[31] It discusses several mining disasters in detail, generally ones where a great loss of life occurred, whilst glossing over other minor incidents. The number of accidents discussed makes explicitly clear how dangerous an industry coal mining was. It gives reasons for accidents and tries to give solutions such as improvement in mine mapping and test drilling for accumulated bodies of water, highlighting again the role of good mining practice and technology. Although occupational disease is not a focus of this study, *Miners Lungs: A History of Dust and Disease in the British Coal Mining Industry,* published in 2007 by McIvor and Johnston, is relevant to understanding the risks of accidents.[32] Their volume discusses the general health of workers in mines and makes it clear what affect inhaling dust had on workers bodies. This is a more recent focus in the literature and raises the question does health have an impact on safety in mines?

---

[30] Annual Reports of the Mines Inspectors, *Parliamentary Papers,* (1872) pp 244
[31] Duckham, B.F & Duckham, H. Great Pit Disasters (1973)

[32] McIvor, A & Johnston, R., *Miners' lungs: a history of dust disease in British coal mining* (Aldershot, 2007)

Theoretically carelessness in the workplace could result from feeling unwell and an associated lack of focus.

Finally there are few studies that detail rates of mortality before the collection of data by the Mines Inspectorate in 1850. Hair's 'Mortality from Violence in British Coal Mines, 1800-1850' published in 1968, is key to this study. His estimates provide the foundations for comparison of mortality before and after the 1850 act.[33] Hair's article also provides information about geological variation between coalmines. For example in the Black Country seams were thick and once the coal was removed the high roofs and sides became unstable, he contrasts this to other districts where seams were narrow. Again this emphasises the role of geological conditions in accident safety raised by Mills above.

This literature review has raised several key issues about why accidents were so common in mines and why they differed between mines. These can be themed as Geology or Fixed Working Conditions, Technology and Human Behaviour and provide the direction and focus for the chapter structure. The chapter on Geological or fixed working conditions examines the role of gas, rock stability, the hazards of working below the water table and atmospheric conditions in the two inspection districts. Chapter three similarly explores the role of technology including the safety lamp, gunpowder, haulage and company size. The final chapter emphasises human behaviour in relation to geology and technology and examines the role of

---

[33] Hair, P.E.H. Mortality from Violence in British Coal Mines, 1800-50, *Economic History Review,* Vol. 21 Issue 3 (December 1968) pp 545-561

masculinity, age and risk taking behaviour. All three chapters are supported by qualitative evidence and statistical data drawn from the inspectors or the period 1877-1887.

In conclusion the research will suggest whilst it is possible to legislate for geological conditions and technological advancement (or lack of) it is not possible to wholly regulate human behaviour. Although conditions between the two districts were different, the potential risk of a fatal accident was not dissimilar, what accounts for the increased mortality in the East was the careless and risky actions of the work force.

Chapter 2: Fixed Working Conditions

This chapter will discuss the impact that geological conditions had on accidents in the mines in the two districts, geological conditions were largely fixed, and had to be worked with, they could not be changed and had to be managed or controlled. These were the factors that predetermined working conditions. Geology fixed the location of the coal mine, its depth, the access, by drift or shaft, the presence of gas, the hardness of the seam and county rock, as well determining accident risk.[34] For example Texture, inclination and faulting of coal seams could all present different hazards.[35] This Chapter will explore both the qualitative and quantitative data contained in the Mines Inspector's reports, in the period under study on fixed working conditions in coal mines, with the circumstances being largely determined by the local geology of coal mines. The chapter will include a discussion of the differing physical attributes of mines in both the West and the East districts, such as the presence of gas and unstable ground, both potentially affected accident rates. Finally the impact that atmospheric conditions had on mines safety will be discussed. The East and West district of Scotland will be placed in the wider British context. The chapter will conclude by suggesting that local geology was a major factor in the differing rates of accident mortality between the two districts.

---

[34] Greasley, D. 'Fifty Years of Coal Mining Productivity: The Record of the British Coal Industry before 1939' *The Journal of Economic History,* Vol. 50, No.4 (December. 1990) p 885
[35] Greasley, D. 'Fifty Years of Coal Mining Productivity: The Record of the British Coal Industry before 1939' *The Journal of Economic History,* Vol. 50, No.4 (December. 1990) p 886

Beginning with the British context, Hair's research was one of the only studies that looked at mortality rates in British coal mines before legislation was brought in. His article makes clear that mortality from roof falls was at its highest in the Black Country. This was due to a physical oddity of the coalfield, and the presence, especially in Dudley, of very thick coal seams that were difficult to manage. These thick seams resulted in high roofs once the coal was removed, and accounted for an abnormal frequency of serious rock falls and therefore a high mortality rate.[36] On the other hand, just as the Black Country was known for its high number of roof falls, the North East coalfield (Durham and Northumberland) were notorious for their underground explosions. This was again due to local conditions, and the extreme gassiness of some of the seams. This caused frequent explosions, many of which led to a heavy loss of life. Towards the end of the eighteenth century, the mines of the North East began to penetrate deeper into gassier seams. A series of disasters promptly followed.[37] Technological responses to accident risk are discussed below in chapter 3. Hair's study makes clear that there was an East/West divide in England due to geology. Does this follow through in the Scottish regions?

If the data for the East of Scotland between 1877-1887 is examined (see graph 2:1 below) it can be seen that explosions contributed hugely to overall mortality rate.[38] The East district witnessed peaks and troughs, years where there were many

---

[36] Hair, P.E.H. 'Mortality from Violence in British Coal-Mines, 1800-50' *The Economic History Review*, New Series, Vol.21, No. 3 (December 1968) p 559
[37] Hair, P.E.H. 'Mortality from Violence in British Coal-Mines, 1800-50' *The Economic History Review*, New Series, Vol.21, No. 3 (December 1968) p 560
[38] Data sourced from Annual Reports of the Mines Inspectors, *Parliamentary Papers*, (1877-1887)

killed due to explosions of firedamp and years where a relatively small number lost their lives. For example in 1877 there were 6 deaths per thousand men and in 1882 there were 5 deaths per thousand men. Whereas in 1886 there were no men killed due to explosions of firedamp and in 1880 there was only 1 death per thousand men.

Graph 2:1

Fatalities due to Explosions of Firedamp (East)

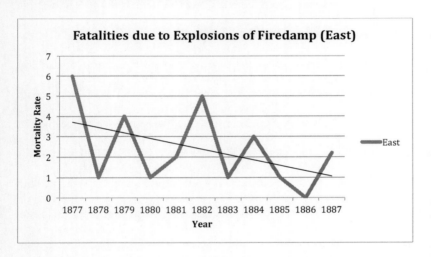

It is clear that the East of Scotland had a high mortality rate due to explosions of firedamp, especially at the beginning of the period under scrutiny. In 1877 the graph shows mortality rates at a peak of six deaths per thousand men. This was due to a great explosion at Blantyre colliery, which killed at least 200 colliers. Blantyre colliery featured heavily in the East districts inspector's (Mr Moore) reports. It is clear that Blantyre was a mine prone to gassiness and explosions. Although after the disaster in 1877 various experiments were conducted, including leaving the mine without ventilation for various time periods. During these experiments no gas could be detected and so Mr Moore's conclusion was that ' the explosion occurred from some abnormal state of matters that certainly did not result from the usual fiery conditions of the mine'.[39] Improvements were made after the incident, including working with the 'long wall' method instead of 'stoop and room',[40] safety lamps were adopted and they stopped using gunpowder in the working of splint coal.[41] However despite all of these measures there was another explosion at Blantyre the following year, this time it was not fatal. Unfortunately a 3rd explosion in 1879 was fatal, all 28 men working underground at the time were killed. The origin of the blast is unknown. Blantyre regularly featured in the Mines Inspectors Reports, with reference to both fatal and non-fatal explosions throughout the period of this study. It should be considered that official statistics for the period between 1850-1885 show that in the United Kingdom there was an annual average of 56 fatal explosions, with the annual average loss of life being 237.[42] So it can be said that there are years where the East of Scotland accounted for a significant proportion of the total number of lives lost. For example, in 1877 fatalities in the East of Scotland accounted for 91% of this total and in 1885, 32% of the total. The addition of a trend line in the graph 2:1 reveals an overall decline over the 10-year period, so whilst this makes it

---

[39] Moore, R. Annual Reports of the Mines Inspectors, *Parliamentary Papers*, (1877) p 135
[40] 'Long wall' was a new method of mining where a 'long wall' of coal is mined in a single slice. 'Stoop and room' was the term generally used in Scotland for this method of mining in which only part of the coal is extracted and pillars of coal are left untouched to support the roof of the seam.
[41] Moore, R. Annual Reports of the Mines Inspectors, *Parliamentary Papers*, (1877) p 135. 'Splint Coal' was a hard, dull, blocky, grayish-black, banded bituminous coal characterized by an uneven fracture and a granular texture; burns with intense heat. Also known as splent coal.
[42] 'Explosions in Coal Mines' *Science,* Vol. 9, No. 222 (May 6, 1887) p 429

clear that safety measures that were put in place reduces the incidents of explosions, it also reveals that a gassy mine will remain hazardous and continue to claim lives.

In comparison, mines in the West of Scotland had far fewer explosions of firedamp, and were less gassy. In the 1886 Mines Inspectors report by Mr Ronaldson, he commented that only 2 mines in the West required safety lamps.[43] That said the West did have some explosions of gas throughout the period under question, with the greatest number occurring in 1878 and 1879. However, explosions in these years, and in the district as a whole, appear to be the result of human error rather than any major occurrence of methane. An example of this comes from the 1877 Mines Inspectors Report, which discusses an explosion at Rosehall colliery near Coatbridge. The deceased had arranged to remove tools belonging to another worker in an area of the mine not being worked. This was in direct violation of the 75th Special Rule of the colliery, which stated 'all workmen are prohibited from entering or remaining in any place throughout the mine where they are not absolutely required to be at the time'.[44] Areas of a colliery that were not being worked were often not ventilated, and accumulations of gas could occur, this posed a hazard. It is also made clear that General Rule number 4 wasn't followed either. This rule demands that management must fence off places 'not in actual work'.[45] The Inspector, Mr Alexander (replaced by Mr Ronaldson on his death in 1885) concludes his report by making it clear that

---

[43] Ronaldson, J. Annual Reports of the Mines Inspectors, *Parliamentary Papers*, (1886) p 301
[44] Alexander, W. Annual Reports of the Mines Inspectors, *Parliamentary Papers*, (1877) p 240
[45] Alexander, W. Annual Reports of the Mines Inspectors, *Parliamentary Papers*, (1877) p 240

this was an entirely preventable accident and blame was shared equally by both miner and management.

At this point it should be noted that there was a school of thought that believed that the Inspectors were on the side of the establishment, and were more likely to blame the workers for accidents. Carson argues that this was true of factory Inspectors; he makes clear there is a 'possibility of bias in the administration of justice'.[46] Although this is an important point to consider it can be said that when it came to Mines Inspectors, the general consensus was that they were committed to safety and were on the side of their miners.[47] Mr Alexander falls into this latter category. He also stated in this report that explosions of firedamp in the West have decreased, mainly due to special rules that related to the fireman's examiner, who was employed to check for gas before work commenced. The examiner must now leave proof of his morning visit to a mine with chalk. Mr Alexander implemented this measure under Special Rules in an attempt to protect the workforce.

---

[46] Carson, W.G. 'White Collar Crime and the Enforcement of Factory Legislation' *British Journal of Criminology*, Vol. 10. No.4 (1970) p 385
[47] Benson, J. *British Coal Miners in the Nineteenth Century* (London, 1980) & Chuch, R. *The History of the British Coal Mining Industry Vol.3: 1830-1913 Victorian Pre-eminence* (Oxford, 1986) & Duncan, R. *The Mine Workers* (Edinburgh, 2005)

Graph 2:2

Fatalities due to Explosions of Firedamp (West)

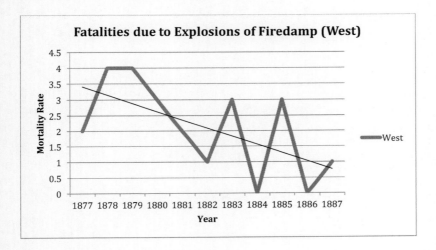

With reference to graph 2.2 as in the East there are also peaks and troughs in the number killed by explosions of firedamp in the West. However, the greatest number killed is not as high as in the East and there are two years where there were no deaths due to explosions of firedamp. Mortality rate never exceeded 4 deaths per thousand men in the West (compared to 6 deaths per thousand men in the East) and it only hit this peak once. Comparison of the two graphs indicates a greater risk of explosion from dangerous gases in the East.

It should also be considered that although combustible gases caused a great number of deaths, suffocation by other dangerous gases such as carbon dioxide and monoxide also posed a threat. The presences of these gasses, particularly carbon monoxide were often the result of the process of combustion. The mortality rate as a result of suffocation by these gases can be seen below. It can clearly be seen in graph 2:3 that there were no instances where miners were suffocated by gases in the West, where as the East does have several years where mortality rates were higher, with the peak deaths being 0.3 deaths per thousand men.

Graph 2:3

Fatalities due to Suffocation by Gases

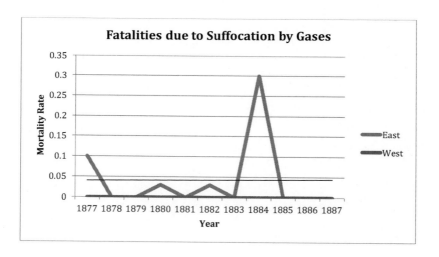

The evidence is clear that the East had far gassier seams than the West and consequently more deaths. This is a fixed working condition that is a by-product of the type of coal mined and how it was originally formed. It is something that cannot be changed, it requires adaption and the introduction of safety measures to minimise the hazards when working the seam. What is particularly revealing is that there is no mention in Mr Moore's Eastern reports of any measures put in place to ensure that the fireman's visit was recorded as was demanded by Mr Alexander in the West. So perhaps safety legislation was taken more seriously in the West. The role of human behaviour will be discussed in further detail in the final chapter.

Despite the fact that mines in the West of Scotland had a reputation for being less gassy they were instead more prone to unstable rock, as discussed in Hairs article above.[48] Hair made it clear that the greater the thickness of the coal seam, the greater the risk of falls of ground. This correlated with the West of Scotland where the seams were also thick. The general rock structure of the west is modified by faulting and by subsidiary folding, the most conspicuous feature of which were the Capsie and Milrigavie – Kilsyth faults, along with the sharp anticlinal ridge known as the 'Riggin' of Kilsyth. The thicknesses of seams in this area vary from 850ft to just over 1300ft. In the Batmore area seam thickness was about 950ft and lastly in Shirva they were around 1380ft.[49] The geological make-up of the Western districts seams resulted in a high mortality rate from falls of ground. In his reports, Mr Alexander, is constantly stating that 'falls of roof and sides could be prevented with a liberal supply of prop wood',[50] and makes it clear that until this happens falls of roof and sides will continue to happen in his district due to the geology of mines.[51] These falls of ground always made up a high percentage of the overall accident mortality rate for the West. In 1882 falls of ground amounted to 60% of all accidents in the district, even when

---

[48] Hair, P.E.H. 'Mortality from Violence in British Coal-Mines, 1800-50' *The Economic History Review,* New Series, Vol.21, No. 3 (December 1968) p 559
[49] Anderson, E. *Economic Geology of the Central Coalfield, Area 1, Kilsyth and Kirkintilloch,* (Edinburgh, 1937) p 5
[50] Alexander, W. Annual Reports of the Mines Inspectors, *Parliamentary Papers,* (1879) p 139
[51] Alexander, W. Annual Reports of the Mines Inspectors, *Parliamentary Papers,* (1879) p 139

accidents were below average in 1883 they still amounted to 42% of all accidents.[52] It should also be noted that in 1886 Mr Ronaldson (Mr Alexander's replacement) noted that 'during the last 14 years there has been no improvements, taking into account the number of persons employed, in reducing falls of ground.'[53] It is therefore clear that improvements needed to be made. Both Mr Alexander and Mr Ronaldson made suggestions, but despite the availability of prop wood workers largely ignored these. It is therefore unclear if improvements in working practices could have overcome abnormal seam thickness and lead to a safer working environment in the West of Scotland.

Access tunnels and roads driven into rock underground were intended to last the lifetime of a mine. A more permanent solution was to use a brick lining, but this was expensive. Colliery owners tended to only brick line immediate area around the shaft bottom and known unstable areas. Unless roads were well constructed and adequately maintained the dangers presented by crush and collapse, as can be seen in the graph 2:4 below, were costly in human life. The use of rock bolts should also be considered as a solution to falls of roofs, they were used as a way to prevent falls of rock from the late 19th century onwards. Rock bolts are long anchor bolts; they transfer the load from the unstable exterior to the confined, stronger interior of the rock.[54] When bolting employed it was a far more effective method of propping than

---

[52] Alexander, W. Annual Reports of the Mines Inspectors, *Parliamentary Papers,* (1883) p 40
[53] Ronaldson, J. Annual Reports of the Mines Inspectors, *Parliamentary Papers,* (1886) p 300
[54] Zhao, Jian & Zhu, Weishen. *Stability Analysis and Modelling of Underground Excavations in Fractured Rocks.* (2003) p 247

by wood. Although rock bolts did present some problems of their own, wood creaked if the load it was supporting was too heavy and was about to fall, whilst steel bolts did not. Nonetheless, bolting when put in place steel was a more effective method. However rock bolts were not introduced until the late 1890s and were not yet an option for colliery safety in the period under study.

Graph 2:4

Fatalities due to Falls in Ground (East)

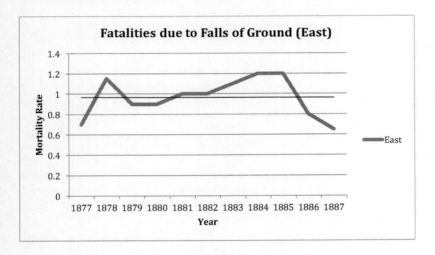

Graph 2:5

Fatalities due to Falls in Ground (West)

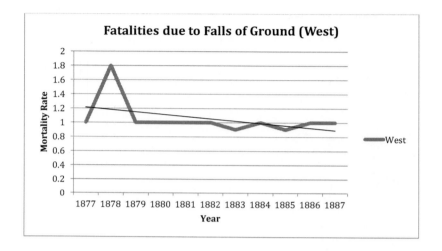

Graphs 2:4 and 2:5 above demonstrate the higher number of fatalities in the West compared to the East. It must be noted however that there was a fairly consistent number of fatalities due to falls of ground in each district, and neither district had a year where there were no deaths due to falls of ground. Therefore it can be suggested that unstable rocks were a problem in both districts. The West however peaks at 1.8 deaths per thousand men in comparison to the Easts' 1.2 deaths per thousand men. The West also had a higher mortality rate in 7 out of the 10 years during the period under examination.

The coal seams in the East district were much narrower and on average the district had fewer fatalities caused by falls of roof. Seam thickness in the Eastern portion of Dunfermline, in Fife was estimated to be around 610ft, this is 300ft less than the narrowest seam in the West. The coal measures near Kincardine did reach a thickness of 1061ft and at Blairhall thickness of 1150ft, was recorded.[55] However, although falls of ground did occur they were less frequent and of a much smaller magnitude. Inspector Moore described the occurrence as 'moderate'.[56] Towards the end of the 19th century Mr Moore urged colliery owner to use methods of propping. This concern appears to be in relation to the hazards of methane. Due to the presence of the gas the mines could only be worked by safety lamps, which at the time gave out a feeble amount of light. Consequently the miners could not observe faults in the ground very easily.[57] Essentially the resolution of one problem created another. Mr Moore's comments in the period primarily relate to the presence of explosive gas, which plagued his district. Falls of ground were not seen as a major source of anxiety.[58] Given the difference in seam thickness and the relationship to accident fatality, this offers an explanation for the differing rates of mortality between the two districts.

A further fixed condition to be considered is inundation or inrushes of water into the underground working environment. Inrushes of water happened due to a number of different factors once coal extraction goes beneath the water table; the geology of the mine, how advanced pumping technology was and poor map keeping. The chief danger of a water inrush always lay in the existence of older, abandoned

---

[55] Haldane. *Economic Geology of the Fife Coalfields area 1 Dunfermline and West Fife,* (Edinburgh, 1931) p 5
[56] Moore,R. Annual Reports of the Mines Inspectors, *Parliamentary Papers,* (1882) p 234
[57] Moore,R. Annual Reports of the Mines Inspectors, *Parliamentary Papers,* (1881) p 314
[58] Moore,R. Annual Reports of the Mines Inspectors, *Parliamentary Papers,* (1882) p 234

workings that had not been mapped or recorded precisely. Early maps, if they were completed, were primitive and often difficult to read or understand. Mapping of mines was made compulsory in 1850. The Inspectors could not obtain copies but could request to view them. This changed in 1872, when the Secretary of State made it compulsory to map a mine within three months of its abandonment and that copies be lodged with the British geological Survey.[59] This compulsory measure under the law may well explain why there were so few deaths due to inrushes of water. See graph 2:6 and 2:7 below. Both the East and West have a peak in fatalities at the beginning of the period under examination. Then there were no more fatalities. This was a safety issue that was targeted early on in the development of legislation. Although not graphed there were also no fatalities due to falling into water in either district, again prevention was an early focus of regulation.

---

[59] Duckam, H & Duckham, B. *Great Bit Disasters,* (Plymouth, 1973) p 25

Graph 2:6

Fatalities due to inrushes of water East

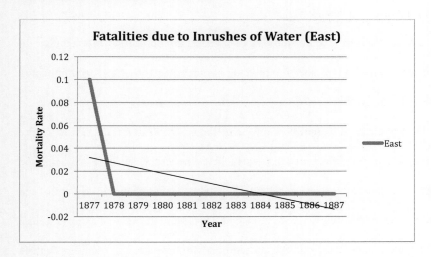

Graph 2:7

Fatalities due to Inrushes of Water (West)

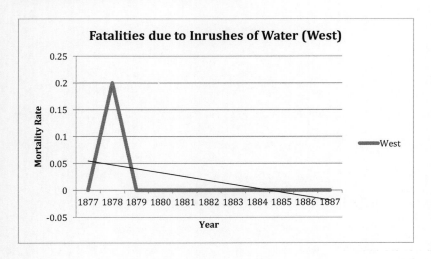

During the long history of coal mining, a belief has developed among miners that mine explosions and roof falls are often associated with stormy weather.[60] Coal mining companies also acknowledge the possibility of such a relationship, to the extent that some colliery owners took extra precautions during stormy weather. In relation to falls of roof this is a myth, however atmospheric conditions are implicated in explosions of methane. Methane expands and contracts with variations in atmospheric pressure and temperature and is mediated by the weather.[61] Air pressure underground varies according to changes in pressure at the surface. Any marked decrease in atmospheric pressure results in an increase in the methane content of the mine air and any marked increase in atmospheric pressure at the surface results in a decrease in the methane content in the underground atmosphere.[62] In contrast changes in surface temperature has very little impact on underground temperature. It is perhaps fortunate that the fiery mines were located in the East of Scotland, which is less prone to stormy weather.

In conclusion, there are various aspects of working conditions that are determined by geology. They are immutable and have to be managed and controlled. Hair's discussion on seam thickness in England has provided the chapter with a foundation, which follows through into the East and West districts of Scotland. The thin seams of the Fife and Clackmannanshire coalfields resulted in fewer falls of roof.

---

[60] McIntosh, C.B. 'Atmospheric Conditions and Explosions in Coal Mines' *Geographical Review*, Vol. 47, No.2 (April, 1957) p 154

[61] McIntosh, C.B. 'Atmospheric Conditions and Explosions in Coal Mines' *Geographical Review*, Vol. 47, No.2 (April, 1957) p 156

[62] McIntosh, C.B. 'Atmospheric Conditions and Explosions in Coal Mines' *Geographical Review*, Vol. 47, No.2 (April, 1957) p 158

In contrast the presence of methane resulted in an increased risk of explosion. Whereas in the West district the opposite is true, the colliers were at greater risk of being crushed or buried alive but were not so exposed to the risk of explosion. There was little difference in the frequency of inrushes of water between the districts, and it is unlikely that atmospheric conditions significantly altered the risk of fatal accidents. Whilst this explains why there might be a difference in accident mortality between the two districts, both were regulated under the same law. What is particularly interesting to note is that protection from inrushes of water was determined by General Rules, whereas falls of roof and side and how fiery mines were managed was regulated by a mix of both General and Special rules. As discussed in chapter one Special Rules were implemented to address local and regional differences in the inspection districts. However, Special Rules were subordinate to the General Rules, they were devised by individual Mines Inspectors and the colliery owners and did not carry the same weight of penalty, i.e. they did not result in prosecution in a court of law. In essence implementation could be obstructed and they were easier to overlook and disobey. This suggests that human behaviour hindered the consistent and stringent regulation of geologically determined hazards.

Chapter 3: Technology

Wyman, in his study of American miners and the industrial revolution draws a direct link between technology and risk[63]. Church discusses the fact that the speed and extent to which technology advanced depended on how effective the administration of the colliery owners were, suggesting that company size was an important factor in the introduction of new innovations.[64] Brown, however, suggests that the bigger mining companies were safer, which directly contradicts Wyman.[65] This chapter will explore technology and company size in relation to accident mortality in the two Scottish districts. It specifically examines fatalities from explosions of gunpowder, fatal accidents caused by the breakage of ropes and chains, accidents in relation to mechanical man haulage and the use of inclined planes. The development of the safety lamp is also briefly discussed. As in previous chapters, a quantitative and qualitative approach is adopted. Innovation in mining practice, equipment and machinery was similarly regulated under Special Rules. Can the same trend that was seen in Fixed Working Conditions, the lack of uniform application of this subordinate body of regulation, be discerned in relation to technology?

The use of gunpowder to bring down coal and for blasting rock to access that coal was well established by the 1870's. Miners would hand make boreholes using

---

[63] Wyman, M. *Hard Rock Epic: Western Miners and the Industrial Revolution, 1860-1910*, (California, 1992)
[64] Church, R. *The History of the British Coal Industry Vol 3, Pre Victorian Eminence,* (New York, 1986) p 386
[65] Brown, R. *Hard Rock Miners: The intermountain West, 1860-1920,* (Texas, 2000)

drills and hammers, usually up to two feet deep and about one inch in diameter. These blast holes would then be charged with powder, and a long, thin 'pricker' would be pressed down the hole. The hole would then be packed with clay, the pricker was then removed and lengths of straw or reed full of fine powder would be inserted to act as a fuse. Touch paper (paper soaked in saltpetre) would be fixed to the end of the straw; the miner would then light it and run. In 1854, T.J Taylor wrote that gunpowder increased the output of hard coal by between 20 and 30%, and so it can be said that although gunpowder blasting was dangerous, particularly before the invention of the safety fuse in 1831, in it was effective in increasing output.[66] However, safety fuses were not widely introduced in coal mining until 1870. These consisted of a tarred rope with a core of powdered gunpowder. It burned at a fixed rate, which would give the miner a better chance escaping the blast. It, however, remained a risky task. Blasting with gunpowder could also ignite methane and cause a gas explosion. Mines Inspectors advised against its use in fiery mines. Consequently, except when blasting hard rock, gunpowder primarily was used in extraction to hew hard coal and only where ventilation was good and where the presence of methane was significantly low. This is a reason why the East had more fatalities due to explosions of gunpowder; see graph 3:1 and 3:2 below. The East had, as previously mentioned, mines that were far more prone to explosions of methane as can be seen in graph 2:1 in the previous chapter. Consequently, there could therefore

---

[66] Taylor, T.J. *RC Accidents*, (London, 1854) p 1094 & Brown, G.I, The big Bang A history of explosives, (Stroud, 1998) p 71

be a link between the number of deaths due to explosions of gunpowder and the fatalities due to explosions of firedamp, as one exacerbates the other. This is a prime example of where the risk of accident is exacerbated by technology combined with fixed working conditions.

Graph 3:1 below illustrates the fatalities due to explosions of gunpowder from 1877 to 1887. Although there are three years during this period where there are no fatalities due to explosions of gunpowder, accidents began to rise again towards the end of the period, although it did not reach the earlier peak of 0.2 deaths per thousand men. This increase is unexpected as expanded legislation was introduced in 1884, to improve the safety of shot firing, which should in theory have further reduced fatalities.[67]

---

[67] Church, R. *The History of the British Coal Industry Vol 3, Pre Victorian Eminence,* (New York, 1986) p 342. Blasting with gunpowder was regulated under a separate body of legislation, 1884, was an amendment of the 1875 Act.

Graph 3:1

Fatalities due to Explosions of Gunpowder (East)

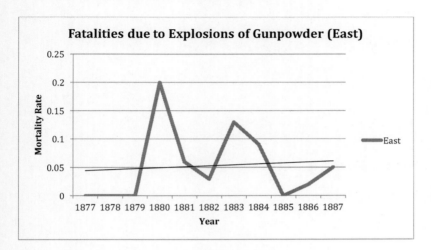

It is therefore worth considering if these increase deaths is perhaps due to human error, given that legislation should have resulted in a level playing field. Were miners in the East district taking more risks when lighting the fuse, or did the company or Mines Inspector not enforce the law? This will be examined in detail in the following chapter. In 1879 the state of blasting practice was examined in some detail by W.Y Craig, (a mine owner in the North Shropshire Coalfield) and the mining inspectorate. These studies provide details of the extent of the use of the gunpowder in the North East of England where 43% of the production was extracted by explosives.[68] In the East of Scotland men favoured the use of gunpowder to minimise physical effort, despite the risks involved. The labour costs of extraction and ultimately the cost of

---

[68] Craig, W.Y. 'Prohibition of blasting in coal mines: its effect on the cost of production' *TWSIME* (1879) pp 53-59

coal would also have increased, if the use of gunpowder had been banned. It was a high price to pay for a reduction in labour and cheap coal.

While the East district had an upward trend toward the end of this period, the West had a downward trend as can be seen from the graph 3:2 below.

Graph 3:2

Fatalities due to Explosions of Gunpowder (West)

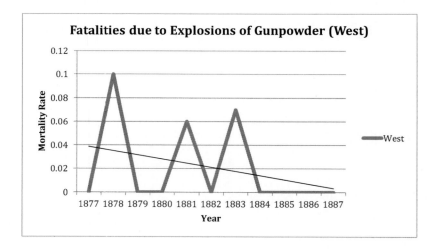

From 1884, a year after legislation was brought in to regulate shot firing there were no deaths from explosions of gunpowder. Moreover, fatalities due to explosions of gunpowder were never higher than 0.1 deaths per thousand men and were consistently lower than that of the East. Although the absence of gunpowder related fatalities directly correlates with the introduction of the new legislation, there were also technological advances around blasting practices introduced around this period.

It should also be considered that from 1880 onwards a variety of new explosives were introduced; notably Bobbinite, an improved 'safety' gunpowder and also the Gelignite/dynamite family of explosives, designed by Nobel. These explosives were more stable and accidental ignition was less likely. They were also more powerful. Gelignite had five times the blasting power of gunpowder and dynamite had three times the power, however all of these new explosives were more expensive. They cost roughly 50% more than gunpowder.

The mines in the West were owned by larger companies with an equally large supply of capital, and as Brown's study revealed the larger the mine the greater its safety provision. It could afford to bear the cost of new safety technology.[69] Company size and its relationship to fatal accidents are discussed in more depth below.

The East of Scotland had 230 firms listed as operating coal mines in 1874. At this point only 15 were limited companies. It was only large firms that were likely to become limited companies. So it can be said that small companies managed the majority of the collieries in the East. This can be seen in Mr Moore's observations in his 1885 Mines Inspector Report, he makes clear that although there were 171 companies engaged in raising coal in his area that year, 53% of the output was raised by 24 firms. The other 147 small companies raised the remaining 57%.[70]

---

[69] Brown, R. *Hard Rock Miners: The intermountain West, 1860-1920,*(Texas, 2000)
[70] Chuch, R. *The History of the British Coal Mining Industry Vol.3: 1830-1913 Victorian Pre-eminence* (Oxford, 1986) p 40

In contrast, the Western district was dominated by a number of large companies, such as the firm of William Baird, which monopolised the West. By 1928 the Company employed 62% of miners in the West district.[71] Although it should be noted, that similar to the East, smaller firms supported the total production of the district. In terms of ownership the East and the West were markedly different, smaller collieries dominated the East, which were run by companies that only operated one mine, whereas the West had large companies that owned several operational mines. This is an important point to consider when it comes to the financial ability to implement technology in mines. The West were more advanced in to terms of how quickly they implemented new measures, and this has a direct corrolation with company size and available capital to implement these changes. The Eastern mines fell behind in certain aspects of technology and this may have been due to there small scale and individual owners, and so lacked the funds to implement major changes as quickly as the West could. This offers another plausible explanation for the Western district having fewer accident fatalities than the East.

In relation to the fatalities involving haulage the Mine Inspectors had three categories; the breakage of ropes and chains, mechanical man haulage and haulage of trams and tubes, i.e. the movement of coal and waste around the mines, and the use of inclined planes. This later two categories relates to the efficient transport of both coal, waste and labour from the working place, along the haulage roads and up the

---

[71] Campbell, A. *The Scottish Miners, 1874-1939. Volume 1, Industry, work and community*, (2000, Aldershot) p 27

shafts (or along the drift) to the surface, and was one of the most important aspects of mining technology. In the early days of mining young boys worked these systems. However, this was banned under the 1842 Mines and Collieries Act and indirectly potentially improved safety by removing children from positions of responsibility.

The first system of mechanised haulage to come into wide use was the main and tail rope, whereby the engine wound two ropes: one hauled the loaded trams to the pit bottom, the other pulled the empty trams in a round pulley at the far end. This system was easy to operate, requiring only a single set of rails. It reached speeds of up to 15 miles per hour, so was quick at transporting coal. However, power consumption was high, which meant the system was expensive to run, wear was considerable and the delivery irregular. The fact that it wore out quickly posed a danger to miners, these early haulage systems did not have brakes, so if ropes snapped, the load they were carrying would topple to the bottom of the pit at high speeds. This created a potential hazard and could kill or maim those workers in its path. The main alternative to this was the use of the 'endless chain system', which was recommended as the cheapest and the safest system by the Tail Rope Committee in 1868.[72] Chains however, were typically heavier than wire ropes and caused additional problems; miners had to be strong enough to man handle the chains successfully. 'Endless chain systems' were eventually replaced with 'endless rope haulage', which was much lighter and the chain system became confined to the

---

[72] Chuch, R. *The History of the British Coal Mining Industry Vol.3: 1830-1913 Victorian Pre-eminence* (Oxford, 1986) p 45

surface, although both systems were very similar, ropes were obviously lighter and easier to work with.

The 'endless systems', despite their safer reputation, was slow to be implemented, and it could be argued that districts which were quicker to switch to this system may have experienced fewer fatalities due to ropes and chains breaking and due to mechanical man haulage. Trams could be attached to the new rope system at various points and the mechanism moved at a walking pace, once clips had been devised to connect tubs securely to ropes and automatic detachers introduced, the use of pulleys and ropes increased this systems efficiency. The explanation for the adoption of this system was the greater regularity of tubs, which facilitated handling. The lightweight and durability of 'the endless rope' system also saved power and maintenance, which in turn saved money. The slower speed of this system also enhanced safety as did the more even spread of the load, and the relatively low labour requirements similarly saved on cost.[73] There were disadvantages like with any system, one of these was that it required twin rails which meant more space was required on underground roads. This problem could be solved with passing places placed at appropriate intervals. From the mid 1870's most new installations used this 'endless rope system', but the working and cost advantage of one system over another does not appear to have been great enough to endure wholesale change at any stage during the period under study. This helps explain why mixtures of technologies

---

[73] Church, R. *The History of the British Coal Industry Vol 3, Pre Victorian Eminence,* (New York, 1986) p 356

were employed at once and so why accident rates varied between collieries and in turn districts. Larger collieries had an advantage as they could absorb the cost of implementing new technologies, whereas smaller collieries often had to make do. A contemporary commentator, Nelson Boyd, regarded the implementation of the endless rope system as the beginning of the general adoption of iron and steel wire rope haulage and hailed it as a great step forward.[74]

The mines inspector's from the period indicate that there was differing levels of technology in terms of haulage implemented in the mines of the East and West of Scotland. Graphs 3:3, 3:4, 3:5 and 3:6 below, depicting a varsity of accidents involving technology, such as ropes and chains support this assertion by revealing differing accident fatality rates in each district.

---

[74] Boyd, N. 'Collieries and colliery engineering' *CG* (Nov, 1893) p 819

Graph 3:3

Fatalities due to Ropes and Chains Breaking (East)

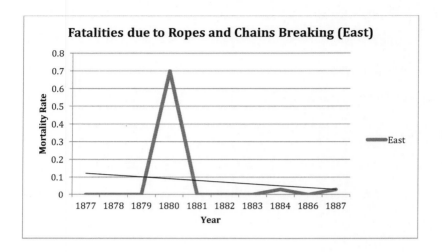

Graph 3:4

Fatalities due to Ropes and Chains Breaking (West)

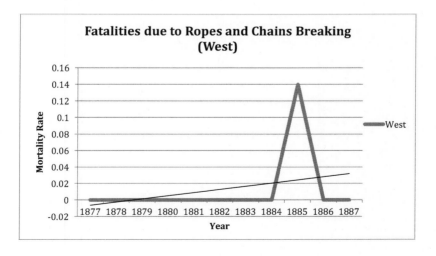

The breakage of ropes and chains was a relatively uncommon occurrence, however both districts reveal an upward trend. The East district has a peak of 0.07 deaths per thousand men over a three-year period. Whereas the West has slightly higher peak of 0.14 deaths per thousand men. However, the West only has one year during time period under examination when there were fatalities. Because of the small numbers of fatalities involved it its difficult to draw any statistically significant conclusions but taken at face value it could indicate a greater level of safety in the mines of the West.

When examining fatalities resulting from mechanical haulage the differences are easier to analyse.

Graph 3:5

Fatalities due to Mechanical Man Haulage (East)

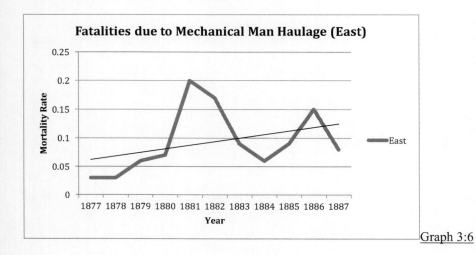

Graph 3:6

Fatalities due to Mechanical Man Haulage (West)

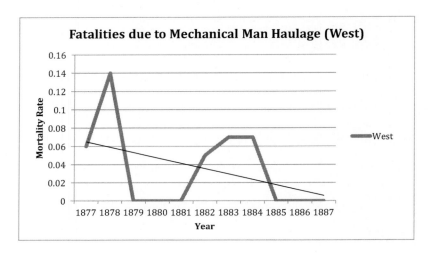

The East has more accidents than the West with its peak at 0.2 deaths per thousand men, whereas the peak in the West is only 0.14 deaths per thousand men. The West also has four years where there were no accidents resulting from haulage. In the East there were fatalities every year. Again this suggests better technology or better maintenance in the West. This contradicts Wyman's assertion that new technology created more hazards and perhaps suggests the technologically backward mines may be less safe or less care was taken in their upkeep.[75]

One aspect of technology that does offer some support for Wyman's argument is the use of the safety lamp. Whilst this innovation is not a focus of the study it would be remiss to fail to discuss its introduction particularly as explosions of methane gas were emphasised in chapter 2. All collieries have struggled to limit or

---
[75] Wyman, M. *Hard Rock Epic: Western Miners and the Industrial Revolution, 1860-1910*, (California, 1992)

prevent explosions in gassy seams. Ventilation was not infallible and the men needed safe illumination to work effectively. Dr Clanny, had developed the idea of isolating a naked flame in a lamp in 1813, and his first lamp designs involved enclosing the flame, and pressurising the lamp via bellows that would use water reservoirs to isolate the flame. The lamp that was developed from these designs was rather clumsy and was of no practical use in the mines. The feature of a glass window, however, would later become a common feature on safety lamps.[76] In 1850 Humphrey Davy also tried to find a way of lighting coal mines safely. The final design was relatively simple, a basic lamp with a wire gauze chimney enclosing the flame. The holes let light pass through, but the metal of the gauze absorbs the heat. The lamp was safe to use because the flame did not produce sufficient heat to ignite flammable gas. The flame itself would change colour if it came into contact with methane and consequently alert the miner to the hazard. The lamp was successfully tested in Hepburn colliery, near Newcastle, in January 1816 and then was quickly put into production. The introduction of the lamp had an immediate affect, decreasing the number of fatalities per million tons of coal produced and it allowed miners to penetrate deeper seams of coal.[77] George Stephenson also developed a lamp, and his principle of leaving space above the flame for 'burnt air' was used in later lamps.

---

[76] McGregor, M. *A Short History of the Scottish Coal Mining Industry* (1958) p 52

[77] McGregor, M. *A Short History of the Scottish Coal Mining Industry* (1958) p 53

Despite aspects of all three men's designs being incorporated into later lamps, Davy's wire gauze principle was used in almost every lamp developed for nearly 200 years.[78]

Whilst the safety lamp reduced the risk of explosion, it encouraged colliery owners to work areas of the mine that were known to be hazardous and illumination was poor compared to candlelight, and reduced visibility carried its own risks.[79] This is a prime example of technology increasing the risk of fatal injury as suggested by Wyman.[80] It may also explain why the gassy East-mining district of Scotland did not adopt safety lamps immediately. Mr Moore, the Mines Inspector for the Eastern District discussed the issue of safety lamps in his 1885 report. He made it clear that safety lamps were now more freely used than they were 7 or 8 years ago, but were still not being used as the sole light source.[81] It is clear from the discussions in chapter two, that until the East of Scotland worked with only safety lamps explosions would continue to happen.

The West however had a more consistent policy on the use of safety lamps, again supporting the idea that they had a more responsible attitude towards safety. However as previously discussed only 2 mines in the West actually required the use of safety lamps, consequently regulations regarding them were far easier to enforce.

---

[78] Church, R. *The History of the British Coal Industry Vol 3, Pre Victorian Eminence,* (New York, 1986) p 60
[79] Hair, P.E.H. 'Mortality from Violence in British Coal-Mines, 1800-50' *The Economic History Review,* New Series, Vol.21, No. 3 (December 1968) p 559 & Mills, C. *Regulating Health and Safety in the British Mining Industries, 1800-1914,* (Surrey, 2010) p 16
[80] Wyman, M. *Hard Rock Epic: Western Miners and the Industrial Revolution, 1860-1910*, (California, 1992)
[81] Moore, R. Annual Reports of the Mines Inspectors, *Parliamentary Papers,* (1885) p 125

Returning to haulage technology, in terms of 'trams' and 'tubes' the comparative rate of accident mortality are depicted below graphs 3:7 and 3:8.

Graph 3:7

Fatalities due to Trams and Tubes (East)

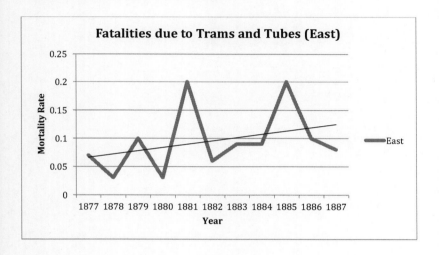

Graph 3:8

Fatalities due to Trams and Tubes (West)

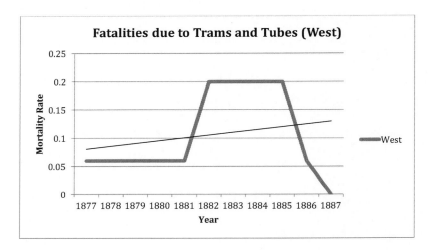

Fatalities in the West due to tram and tube accidents remained on an even trend until 1881, they peaked at 0.2 deaths per thousand men for four consecutive years before declining to zero deaths per thousand men in 1887. The East district witnessed peaks and troughs across the same period. Although the number of fatalities similarly declined towards the end of the period, they remained 0.08 deaths per thousand men. This variation in mortality reflects the variety of different haulage methods used in use as discussed previously. The trend of decline towards the end of the period reflects the introduction of the 'endless rope system', which included a secure tube connection and slower speed.

In the West, across all three categories of haulage fatalities the number of deaths declined towards the end of the period under study. Suggesting a correlation between technological advance and safety. The opposite can be said for the East district, although fatalities in all three categories declined, they did not achieve a perfect success rate. This section has made a link between all three accident categories and provided evidence as to why differing levels of fatalities exist due to variations in the implementation of new technology.

Inclined planes were a sloped surface or ramp in which trams and tubes were moved by gravity, i.e. the weight of a full tube traveling down hill pulled an empty tube uphill. They were essentially steeply graded railways that used a cable or rope wound around a winch system. A stationary engine powered some planes. The speeds of the wagons on the powered plane were controlled by a brake that acted on the winding drum at the top of the slope; there were no brakes on a self-acting plane. If it was necessary to halt a tube then the machine operator would ram a metal bar or a stick of wood through the wheels of the tube. This was clearly risky but there were many other associated hazards, such as collisions, derailing or wagons failing to stop. Slips and falls were a regular occurrence, as was the possibility of a miner hitting their head on a low roof whilst either traveling on or operating the machinery. Despite the dangers that could occur due to these systems, there were very few alternatives that could be employed to combat the issue of haulage where the ground was neither horizontal nor vertical.

With regards to fatalities associated with inclined planes (see graphs 3:9 and 3:10 below) both the East and the West district had peaks of up to 0.2 deaths per thousand men. Whilst the West achieved several years where there were no fatalities, the East witnessed consistent deaths year on year. Both graphs however show an upward trend and it is clear that the use of inclined planes posed a risk to life in both districts. It is interesting that there were no technological advances in safety provision for operating inclined planes.[82] This adds weight to the argument that technology improves safety. Without advances in design and operation even the West district fails to improve its record.

Graph 3:9

Fatalities due to Inclined Planes (East)

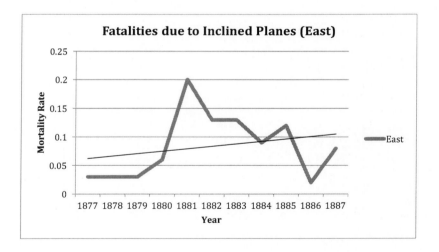

---

[82] Church, R. *The History of the British Coal Industry Vol 3, Pre Victorian Eminence,* (New York, 1986) p 53

Graph 3:10

Fatalities due to Inclined Planes (West)

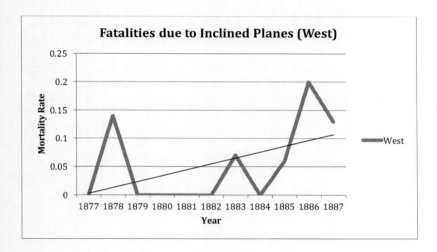

In conclusion, this chapter has discussed a variety of technological innovations. The variation in introduction and application across the two districts has contributed to the differing rates of accident mortality. The varying ways that gunpowder was used was the first aspect of technology in mines that was discussed, and a link was made between the number of fatalities due to explosions of firedamp and its relationship to the use gunpowder. The fact that the 'endless rope system' was implemented in some mines and not others due to cost implications resulted in an advantage in terms of safety. Inclined planes remained hazardous across the period, less emphasis was placed on this due to the fact that there was very little that mine owners could do to combat the problem during this studies time period. The miner's safety lamp was not universally adopted in the fiery Eastern district. The evidence from the Mines Inspectors reports show that the West was clearly paving the way in terms of implementing new and innovative technology, and contradicting Wyman's assertion it had a better safety record than the East, which remained technologically backward.[83] Moreover, large-scale companies operated the West, which supports Brown's suggestion that company size was important in reducing hazards.[84] As with chapter two on fixed working conditions these factors all explain why the West may have a better safety record than the East, but once again this does not fully resolve the question of why should accident rates differ when both districts were regulated by the same law? As with regional variation in geological conditions, Special Rules also attempted to address differences in working practices and technological application.

---

[83] Wyman, M. *Hard Rock Epic: Western Miners and the Industrial Revolution, 1860-1910*, (California, 1992)
[84] Brown, R. *Hard Rock Miners: The intermountain West, 1860-1920*, (Texas, 2000)

Chapter 4: Human Behaviour

Throughout the study so far there have been many references to human error. This final chapter will bring all of these instances together and discuss to what extent they contributed to the overall accident rate. The role of human behaviour is explored in relation to fixed working conditions, technology and defiance of the law. This is followed by an examination of risk taking behaviour and the link between age and accident frequency. What becomes clear is that human error plays a significant role in exacerbating what is already a risky occupation.

The presence of methane is a fixed geological condition that was largely out with the miner's control. It required careful management both in terms of safety provision, i.e. ventilation and the use of miner's lamps and the behaviour of the work force. There are, however, a significant number of explosions of firedamp that were due to lack of care and therefore could have been avoided. An example of this occurred in the West district of Scotland in 1877 at Rosehall Colliery near Coatbridge. The deceased had arranged to remove tools belonging to another worker in an area of the mine not being worked (and consequently not ventilated) and an explosion occurred. This was in direct violation of the 75th Special Rule of the colliery. As discussed above in chapter two, this is a clear example of a miner ignoring a rule set out for his own and the safety of his fellow workers. Mr Alexander, the Inspector, concluded in his report on the death that it was an entirely preventable accident.[85] This is an instance that is again repeated in 1878. Moreover, throughout the period under study in both districts, there were numerous explosions of firedamp resulting from defiance of the Special Rules.[86] This suggests that human negligence exacerbated the risk posed by geologically determined conditions of mines. If a mine did not contain firedamp, human error could not ignite it, a combination of gassy seams and miners ignoring rules was lethal even in technologically advanced mines. This mixture of negligent behaviour and the presence of methane, even in the West district, that was far less gassy, still posed a risk. Five out of the six explosions of methane, during the period under study, that took place in Ayrshire, which was the least fiery area of the West district, involved human error.[87] This indicates how significant the adoption of safe working practice needed to be.

Company fines were the punishment for violating special rules, this however did not appear to make any significant difference to the behaviour of the men. The mining company enforced the rules and the Mines Inspectors were reliant upon the company voluntarily reporting violations, and subsequent fines to them. Consequently it is difficult to assess the true extent of both the enforcement and the defiance of the Special Rules. Violations were only exposed when rule breaking resulted in injury. Fitzpatrick in his participant observation study of an underground mine suggests that a 'subculture of danger' existed in mines. Essentially exposure to

---

[85] Annual Reports of the Mines Inspectors *Parliamentary Papers*, (1877) p 63
[86] Annual Reports of the Mines Inspectors *Parliamentary Papers*, (1878) p 113
[87] Annual Reports of the Mines Inspectors *Parliamentary Papers*, (1880) p 130

hazards created knowledge of dangers that miners became all too familiar with. They learnt the triggers that could lead to accidents and the frequency of occurrence.[88] Heinrich's accident triangle, developed in the 1930s, states that for every fatal accident there are 29 accidents that cause minor injuries, and 300 accidents that cause no injuries.[89] This suggests that fatalities were rare. This rarity of fatal injury according to Fitzpatrick leads to workers developing patterns of protective behaviour and not preventative behaviour.[90] Unsafe working practices continued as workers were aware that they could get away with taking risks, without adverse consequences for the majority of the time.[91] Coopers later article on 'Safety Behaviour' supports Heinrich's earlier findings, making it clear that miners continued to behave in an unsafe way as reckless acts rarely result in injury.[92] Evidence of this can be seen from the fact that attitudes towards safety in the period under examination did not improve, for example this is supported by the explanations for explosions that occurred in 1881 and 1882 in both districts. In 1881, a miner went into an abandoned mine full of debris and inadvertently ignited firedamp. The fireman, who should have checked for the presence of gas before the commencement to work, admitted that he hadn't been in this part of the mine for some days prior to the explosion; he was charged for his negligence. In 1882 another explosion occurred in an abandoned mine, workers had

---

[88] Fitzpatrick, 'Adapting to danger, a Participant observation study of an underground mine', *Sociology of Working Occupation*, Vol 7, No 2, (1980) pp 131-58
[89] Heinrich, H.W. *Industrial Accident Prevention: A scientific approach,* (1931) p 25
[90] Fitzpatrick, 'Adapting to danger, a Participant observation study of an underground mine', *Sociology of Working Occupation*, Vol 7, No 2, (1980) pp 131-58
[91] Heinrich, H.W. *Industrial Accident Prevention: A scientific approach,* (1931) p 25
[92] Cooper, D. 'Casual influences on people's safety behaviour', *Health and Safety in Metals and Metallurgy,* (London, 1996) p 25

wandered in as it was not properly fenced off, as was required by General Rule 4 and Special Rule 28, the over man was charged with negligence in this instance.[93] Towards the end of the period under study the number of fatal accidents due to explosions of methane did begin to decline, however the few accidents that continued to occur were still related to human behaviour, such as in 1887. Again the accident was a result of a miner entering workings where he should not have been.[94] A clear pattern is evident; rules were often ignored, despite there being penalties being in place. Human error seriously increased the risk of fatal injury in the working environment.

Human error also exacerbated the risk of injury from falls of roof and side. Although this risk was linked to the thickness of seams,[95] there were methods that could have been used to minimise the number of falls. These included propping sides with wood and later on rock bolting, as mentioned in chapter 2. The Mines Inspectors in both districts made it explicitly clear that propping was a necessity. Mr Alexander, for example, made calls for this on a regular basis. In his 1879 report he commented that 'falls of roof and sides could have been prevented with a liberal supply of prop wood'.[96] Mr Ronaldson, who took over from Mr Alexander in 1885, noted in 1886 that 'during the last 14 years there has been no improvements, in reducing falls of

---

[93] Annual Reports of the Mines Inspectors *Parliamentary Papers,* (1881) p 197
[94] Annual Reports of the Mines Inspectors *Parliamentary Papers,* (1882) p 112
[95] Hair, P.E.H. 'Mortality from Violence in British Coal-Mines, 1800-50' *The Economic History Review,* New Series, Vol.21, No. 3 (December 1968) p 559
[96] Alexander, W. Annual Reports of the Mines Inspectors, *Parliamentary Papers,* (1879) p 139

grounds'.[97] Although this trend is perhaps not an explicit example of human error in all cases, a clear solution to reduce the risk was set out by the Mines Inspectors, and these were in many cases ignored. Again this reveals the role of human behaviour in safety, and may in part explain why mines in Scotland and elsewhere remained dangerous.

As discussed in chapter 3 above, the men employed the use of gunpowder to minimise the physical effort of extracting coal. If a miner cut the fuse too short, this would reduce his escape time. If he was caught in the blast the injuries could be disabling, such as the loss of eyes or limbs, or at worst death. It is clear from the Mines Inspectors reports that many fatalities due to the use of gunpowder were a result of poor judgment in calculating a safe length of fuse. This hazard was not fully resolved until legislation, as discussed above; on shot firing was passed in 1884. A more pressing concern, in relation to human error and advancing mining technology, are associated with mechanical man haulage. Mechanical man haulage was essentially the movement of men and materials from the pit floor to ground level. In their enthusiasm to escape the underground environment and return home, men overloaded or rode on the outside of cages. Men even demonstrated a curious habit of sticking out arms and legs, and on some occasions even sticking out their heads. This

---

[97] Ronaldson, J. Annual Reports of the Mines Inspectors, *Parliamentary Papers,* (1886) p 300

is an example of men taking unnecessary risks that could lead to injury and even death.[98]

Following on from this it is worth considering the idea of masculinity in the mining environment. As can be seen from above, men clearly had opportunities to break the law and engage in dangerous and risky behaviours. It is therefore worth investigating what motivated this behaviour. As early as 1871 the idea of men taking pride in their ability and strength was being investigated, and it was made clear that men 'delighted in any opportunity to display this'.[99] McIvor and Johnston have investigated this idea and suggested that in a working environment where traditions of 'machismo' predominated, workers would be exposed to peer pressure and management expectations to tolerate high levels of risk.[100] The same is true for peer pressure, many miners preferred the gunpowder method as it required less effort, those who may have been worried by the risk involved would have been coerced into it by their co-workers to save time and effort. Benson emphasises that bullying, quarrelling and intimidation of other miners was common, with owners often turning a blind eye to it. He also makes it clear that time and again miners, particularly the young or inexperienced, diced with both their own lives and with their colleague's

---

[98] Mills, C. *Regulating Health and Safety in the British Mining Industries, 1800-1914,* (Surrey, 2010) p 238
[99] *Mining Magazine and Review,* 1 (January – June 1871) p 138
[100] Johnston, R. & McIvor, A. *Lethal Work: A History of the Asbestos Tragedy in Scotland,* (East Linton, 2000) p 220

lives.[101] An example of managerial pressure was the coercion to use gunpowder, despite its risks, to maximise productivity for the lowest price.

However despite this risk the bodies ability to labour was often the only asset of working class men in the nineteenth century, and many would willingly accept working practices that damaged their bodies as their way of showing they were masculine, and claiming some level of self-respect in the world of wage labour.[102] Following on from this there are legendary tales of heroism in coal mines, some show the desire to be considered masculine, and others were linked to religious beliefs. There is one account of a man sacrificing himself for his partner, as he was perfect in the faith that he would go to heaven if he died.[103] In what was a highly competitive working environment, rivalry was intense and these acts of bravado helped some workers maintain their reputation and their notions of masculinity. The men themselves however, claimed that it was simply, 'youth and inexperience' that accounted for their cavalier attitude towards danger. When older men were fatally injured it was often linked to the indiscretion or ignorance of their younger colleagues.[104] This link with accident frequency and age will be discussed further on in this chapter.

The idea that desire to be considered masculine had an effect on working practices is further supported by McIvor and Johnston's study of masculinity in the

---

[101] Benson, J. *British Coalminers in the Nineteenth Century: A Social History*, (Dublin, 1980) pp 36-37
[102] Connell, R.W. *The Men and the Boys*, (Cambridge, 2000) p 188
[103] Litchfield, J. *Cornwall Its Mines and its Miners*, (London, 1857) pp 292-3
[104] Blee, R. 'On Comparative Health and Longevity of Cornish Miners' *Annual Reports RCPS* (1971) p 54

Clyde side heavy industries. They suggested that a 'cut of toughness' characterised industry on the Clyde, and young male workers adapted to this and absorbed it through peer pressure.[105] Scottish mining communities had long been infused with the idea of manliness, and male youths were encouraged by older miners to avoid displaying emotion (such as crying) and to play fighting games. It was thought this was the training that would teach them to be hard men, which would serve them well in the mines. Dangerous, dirty, dusty and physically exhausting work was associated with coal mines and the constant stream of injuries hardened boys quickly, this in turn desensitised them to danger and associated them with a competitive, macho environment. Any sign of weakness, emotion or vulnerability could lead to them being the butt of jokes, harsh banter and being given scathing nicknames.[106] This in turn led to young boys taking more risks to appear manly, explaining why the mortality rate in relatively young workers was so high, see graph 4:1 below. A competitive spirit it seemed was an essential part of the work culture present in the mines, as was a high tolerance to danger and propensity to take risk. The Mines Inspectors reports detail many instances of miners being killed due to undercutting seams too deep or failing to support their work area properly.[107] Mills's backs this up in her study on Cornish miners, making it clear that individual acts of unsafe practice and defiance of the law were often only uncovered during routine inspections ,and the

---

[105] McIvor, A. & Johnston, R. 'Dangerous Work Hard men and Broken Bodies: Masculinity in the Clyde side Heavy Industries c.1930-1970.' *Labour History Review,* Vol 69, No 2, 2 August 2004
[106] McIvor, A. & Johnston, R. 'Dangerous Work Hard men and Broken Bodies: Masculinity in the Clyde side Heavy Industries c.1930-1970.' *Labour History Review,* Vol 69, No 2, 2 August 2004 p 139
[107] Annual Reports of the Mines Inspectors, *Parliamentary Papers,* (1877-1887)

Mines Inspectors reports across the 19th century are littered with comments such as 'constantly ignores', and 'recklessness of the person injured'.[108] This in turn makes clear that the risky behaviour of miners was not just a problem in Scotland but was more widespread, highlighting that masculinity leading to human error was a major issue in the mining community. In an interview given by a 76 year old retired miner, he recalls how it was the accepted practise not to put in the necessary number of wooden supports: 'Well, you've supposed to put your wood up at a certain time and a certain measurement and all that, that didnae happen, never.'[109] This is a first hand account again making explicitly clear that rules were being ignored. The inherent dangers and harsh, brutal realities of the Clydeside heavy industries acted as a catalyst for the formation of masculinity, these machismo attitudes were formed in almost exclusively male, tough, physically demanding work culture. Which in turn glorified the ability to survive in filthy, brutal mines. It can be said that young men were indoctrinated into believing that taking risks and facing danger would make them seem more masculine. This led to a number of accidents that could have easily been prevented if safe working practices had been followed by miners, and enforced more stringently by mine managers.

It is worth considering if this effect wore off as the miners aged and grew wise to the real dangers of underground work place, or if this macho attitude was a

---

[108] Mills, C. *Regulating Health and Safety in the British Mining Industries, 1800-1914*, (Surrey, 2010) p 236
[109] SOHOPH, *Interview C7* in McIvor, A. & Johnston, R. 'Dangerous Work Hard men and Broken Bodies: Masculinity in the Clyde side Heavy Industries c.1930-1970.' *Labour History Review,* Vol 69, No 2, 2 August 2004

problem into old age. The following four graphs (4:1, 4:2, 4:3, and 4:4) examine the relationship between age and accident frequency, in 1877, 1878, 1885 and 1886.[110] These four years were selected randomly between 1877 and 1887, the period under scrutiny. In each year, fatalities peak in both districts in the age 20 plus category and in the age 50 plus category, whereas middle-aged miners were less at risk of fatal accidents. This suggests that miners were more likely to be killed in their youth and in their older years, This fits comfortably with the hypothesis that people are reckless in their youth and set in their ways in their older years, both of which could lead to a higher rate of fatalities. There are some exceptions in both districts, but even then fatalities are higher at one end of the spectrum than the other. An example of this is 1886, where fatalities in both districts fell in the 50 plus category, which doesn't fit the overall trend. However, fatalities in teens and age 20 categories are still high. Although rates of fatalities fall dramatically after the age of 60, it should be noted that there were very few miners in that age group still at work in the mines.

---

[110] These graphs have been calculated as a percentage, opposed to a mortality rate.

Graph 4:1

% Killed with Reference to Age (1877)

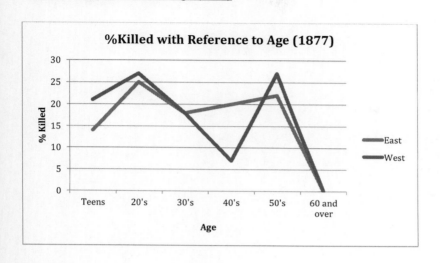

Graph 4:2

% Killed with Reference to Age (1878)

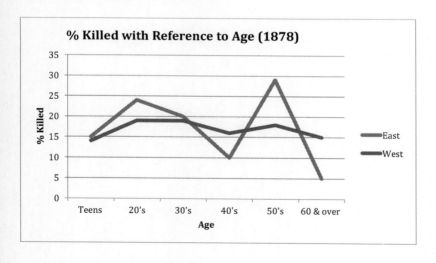

Graph 4:3

% Killed with Reference to Age (1885)

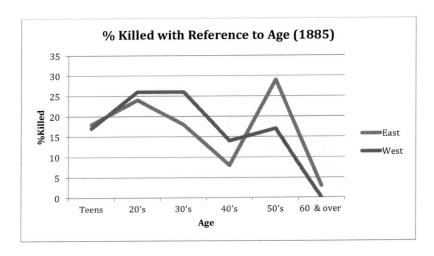

Graph 4:4

% Killed with Reference to Age (1886)

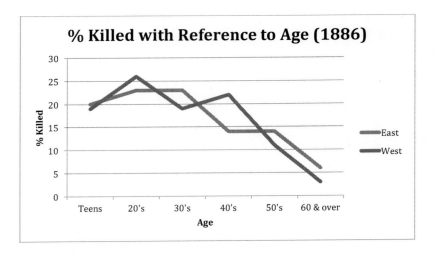

This relationship between age and accident frequency is discussed in detail in Mills's short article examining 'Age and Accident Frequency in Cornish Mining'.[111] Where Mills bases her study on Annual Reports of the Mines Inspectors to create graphs. Her analysis reveals a similar trend. It is made clear that the risk of fatal injury initially peaked in younger men of 21-30 years, and declined with increasing maturity. This trend was dramatically interrupted by a peak of fatal injuries amongst 51-60 year olds.[112] Therefore, the trend revealed in the Scottish districts is reflected elsewhere. However, it is worth considering why this pattern was so consistent throughout Britain. The common belief is that risk of fatal injury peaks in the younger years and then declines with increasing maturity and wisdom. However, the increase in deaths in the older age group refutes this idea. It could be argued that the greater risk of injuries resulting in death amongst the 51-60 year old category, may reflect the bodies declining ability to survive trauma as the body ages, and also the fact that these men were more likely to be in poor health from a working life time exposure to dust and repetitive movements, cramped conditions and poor air quality, as was discussed in chapter one. It should also be considered that these older miners' reaction times were not as quick as their younger counterparts. In addition these men may have acquired potentially dangerous time and labour saving methods that were to compensate for their slower work rate. Older men regularly requested a greater speed of ascent when it came to mechanical man haulage and this led to more

---

[111] Mills.C. 'Does Familiarity Breed Contempt? Age and Accident Frequency in Cornish Non-Ferrous Metal Mining, 1881-1901' *British Mining*, No 75 pp 58-63
[112] Mills.C. 'Does Familiarity Breed Contempt? Age and Accident Frequency in Cornish Non-Ferrous Metal Mining, 1881-1901' *British Mining*, No 75 p 61

accidents.[113] Again this links into the idea of masculinity, older workers may not want to appear unable to do their work as quickly or efficiently as their younger counterparts. The notion of wanting to appear 'macho' is a hazard for miners throughout their working lives. All of these points link into the fact that human error, especially for those men in their advancing years, can lead to dangerous working practices and in turn cause more deaths. As can be seen from the above graphs the number in the final 60 years of age and over category was always extremely small, this reflects the fact that few miners continued to have the strength to work in the collieries by this age, and accounts for the downwards trend in this age category.

Whilst the behaviour of the men and there managers has been explored, it is worth considering the role of the Mines Inspectors. These men implemented the law and also devised the Special Rules, and different men regulated the two districts. In terms of their qualifications the home office stipulated and standardised these, and both Mr Moore and Mr Alexander had similar lengths of service. They were experienced men and neither was ever reprimanded by the Chief Inspector of Mines. It is unlikely that the Wests superior safety record was due to the appointment of the younger and perhaps more enthusiastic and motivated Mr Ronaldson, as his appointment came at the end of the period under study. Quantifying the Inspectors actions is almost impossible. However, Moore's reports lack the depth and detail of Alexander's. For example, Moore would simply provide the statutory list of data in terms of accident reports, whereas Alexander would go beyond his required duties

---

[113] Mills, C. *Regulating Health and Safety in the British Mining Industries, 1800-1914*, (Surrey, 2010) p 239

and provide extra detail.[114] However, there is no evidence to suggest the law was not fully implemented and upheld equally in both districts.

In conclusion, this chapter brings together the previous themes of technology and fixed working conditions, and discusses accident safety under the category the themes of human behaviour. It makes clear that although explosions of firedamp were in some ways determined by the geological makeup of the mine, however, in many instances they could have been avoided if better care and attention by miners and there managers had been taken. The numbers of reports of both the Special and the General Rules that were being ignored indicated that there was a significant level of risk taking. This indicates that human behaviour played a significant role in exacerbating the risk of methane ignition. The same was true when falls of grounds and sides were examined. Mines Inspectors were constantly making clear that if propping and support was employed on a regular basis these accidents could be avoided. Again the work force and their managers exhibited risky behaviour. By drawing upon both Fitzpatrick's and Heinrich's studies, it can be seen that the low frequency of fatal accidents meant that men became all too familiar with the dangers of underground labour and continued to take risks. The idea of masculinity reinforcing and enhancing the men's behaviour, appears to have played a substantial role in accidents in the work place. This, together with the fact that very young and old men were more likely to be killed in mines, made for a dangerous occupation.

---

[114] Alexander, W. Annual Reports of the Mines Inspectors, *Parliamentary Papers,* (1883) p 40 & Moore,R. Annual Reports of the Mines Inspectors, *Parliamentary Papers,* (1882) p 234

These factors, in part, explain why coal mines had differing accident rates in the 19th Century, despite being regulated under the same law and highlights the difficulty of legislating human behaviour.

Conclusion

Coal mining was a risky occupation. Miners were exposed to numerous hazards such as exposure to suffocating and explosive gases; unstable rock; rising water levels; poor ventilation; dust; uneven work surfaces; the use of explosives; fast moving machinery and unreliable ropes and chains. Labour was arduous, repetitive and often undertaken in cramped, hot, damp and unsanitary conditions that were poorly illuminated. In the mid 19th Century life expectancy for a coal miner was 36 years.[115] From 1842 legislation was introduced, that indirectly, and directly from 1850 onwards, regulated accident safety in the collieries. The law stipulated a set of General Rules applicable to all mines across Great Britain and Ireland and to compensate for regional variations in geology and working practises, a set of Special Rules. In theory this should have created a level playing field across the country in terms of safety. As discussed in chapter one, legislation did reduce the overall risk of accident fatality but regional variations in frequency persisted. This variation in rates of accidents can be explained as previously stated by a large body of literature on the subject of coal mines and coal mining accidents. This covers a wide range of subjects from production to the social history of the miners. Whilst specific studies on accident safety are minimal they have provided shape and direction to this study, particularly in relation to the role of geology, technology, age and a machismo

---

[115] See chapter one p 2

working culture[116] and there relationship to risk and safe working practice. It is these factors that help explain the differences in accident mortality across the East and West districts of Scotland despite regulation under the same law.

The second chapter examined fixed working conditions; the characteristics of a mine determined by local and or regional geology such as the presence of methane gas and unstable rock. The chapter on technology went on to discuss the impact that varying levels of technology had on accident rates in coal mines. The East district of Scotland was fiery; methane gas generally present underground but the country rock was stable, and coal seams were narrower which resulted in lower and better naturally supported roofs during and after the extraction of coal. In contrast, the West district was less gassy and had much thicker coal seams, which resulted in unstable roofs and sides. In terms of technology the West district was more advanced than the East, but accidents directly involving technology were greater for the East. This refutes Wyman's argument that technology increases accident risk, but Browns argument that larger companies were safer to work for is upheld. The West district, which overall was the safer of the two districts, had greater company size.[117]

Whilst fixed working conditions, technological advance and company size all affect the frequency of accidents, these factors do not fully explain the difference in

---

[116] Hair, P.E.H. 'Mortality from Violence in British Coal-Mines, 1800-50' *The Economic History Review,* New Series, Vol.21, No. 3 (December 1968) & McIvor, A. & Johnston, R. 'Dangerous Work Hard men and Broken Bodies: Masculinity in the Clyde side Heavy Industries c.1930-1970.' *Labour History Review,* Vol 69, No 2, 2 August 2004 & Mills.C. 'Does Familiarity Breed Contempt? Age and Accident Frequency in Cornish Non-Ferrous Metal Mining, 1881-1901' *British Mining,* No 75

[117] Brown, R. *Hard Rock Miners: The intermountain West, 1860-1920,* (Texas, 2000) & Wyman, M. *Hard Rock Epic: Western Miners and the Industrial Revolution, 1860-1910,* (California, 1992)

mortality rates between the two districts when both were regulated under the same law. Explanations for this inconsistency can be found in human behaviour. Human error was implicated in many of the accidents involving fixed working conditions and technology but the competitive, macho nature of the underground working environment exacerbated existing dangers and resulted in unnecessary risks. In addition a link between the miner's ages and accident rates was also established. In essence the law was a blunt instrument, it did not address differing working cultures and it is this omission that explains the differing accident rates.

The World Coal Organisation makes clear that deep coal mining underground involves a high safety risk. This is due to problems associated methane and the potential for the collapse of roof and sides. The risks that the 19th century miner faced are still present today. There have however been significant advances in health and safety legislation. This alongside better education and training for the underground work force has resulted in improved mining practices.[118] The mortality rate in the UK averages out as 0.25 accidents per thousand men per annum.[119] This is significantly lower than in the 19th century. However, in terms of human behaviour nothing changes. Even though coal mining has virtually declined in Britain, in September 2011 four miners drowned following an inrush of water at Gleision Drift mine in the Swansea valley.[120] They were working in an unauthorised coal rich section of the

---

[118] World Coal Mining Organisation, <http://www.worldcol.org/coal-society/safety-issues/>[Accessed 17/02/2015]
[119] Hazards magazine, issue. 116, (October-December 2011)
[120] Hazards magazine, issue. 116, (October-December 2011)

seam. In October of the same year the mine manager was arrested by south wales police on suspicion of manslaughter.[121] This is an example of poor management and defiance of now much stricter laws, 123 years after this studies time period.

This behaviour is not restricted solely to the UK. An explosion at Greymouth, New Zealand in 2010 proves that lessons have still not been learned. There was evidence of men smoking in the mine, ventilation doors were not properly maintained, the firemen were not measuring methane levels before work began and there were no contingency plan for dealing with fire.[122]

It remains very difficult to legislate for random acts of careless behaviour and even more difficult to change working cultures even today. Scottish coal mining has always been an inherently dangerous industry, and geology and technology do play an important part in this, but the overriding hazard is the miners themselves.

---

[121] Hazards magazine, issue. 116, (October-December 2011)
[122] *Pike River, A failure to Learn,* Produced by the Mines institute of Australia, PYT limited (2014)

Bibliography

Primary Sources

Annual Reports of the Mines Inspectors, *Parliamentary Papers,* (1877-1887)

Boyd, N. *Coal Mines Inspection, Its History and Results* (London, 1879)

Craig, W.Y. 'Prohibition of blasting in coal mines: its effect on the cost of production' *TWSIME* (1879)

'Explosions in Coal Mines' *Science,* Vol. 9, No. 222 (May 6, 1887)

Litchfield, J. *Cornwall Its Mines and its Miners,* (London, 1857)

Mining Magazine and Review, 1 (January – June 1871)

Royal Commission on the Employment of Women and Children in mines, *Parlimentary Papers,* 1942

Taylor, T.J. *RC Accidents,* (London, 1854)

Secondary Sources

Anderson, E. *Economic Geology of the Central Coalfield, Area 1, Kilsyth and Kirkintilloch,* (Edinburgh, 1937)

Benson, J. *British Coal Miners in the Nineteenth Century* (Dublin, 1980)

Benson, J & Neville, R. *Bibliography of the British Coal Industry,* (Oxford, 1981)

Blee, R. 'On Comparative Health and Longevity of Cornish Miners' *Annual Reports RCPS* (1971)

Brown, R. *Hard Rock Miners: The intermountain West, 1860-1920,*(Texas, 2000

Boyd, N. 'Collieries and colliery engineering' *CG* (Nov, 1893)

Bryan, A. *The Evolution of Health and Safety in Mines* (1975)

Bulman H.F., *Coal Mining and the Coal Miner* (London, 1920)

Campbell, A. *The Scottish Miners, 1874-1939. Volume 1, Industry, work and community,* (2000, Aldershot)

Carson, W.G. 'White Collar Crime and the Enforcement of Factory Legislation' *British Journal of Criminology,* Vol. 10. No.4 (1970)

Chuch, R. *The History of the British Coal Mining Industry Vol.3: 1830-1913 Victorian Pre-eminence* (Oxford, 1986)

Connell, R.W. *The Men and the Boys,* (Cambridge, 2000)

Cooper, D. 'Casual influences on people's safety behaviour', *Health and Safety in Metals and Metallurgy,* (London, 1996)

Duckham, B.F & Duckham, H. Great Pit Disasters (1973)

Duncan, R. *The Mine Workers* (Edinburgh, 2005)

Fitzpatrick, 'Adapting to danger, a Participant observation study of an underground mine', *Sociology of Working Occupation,* Vol 7, No 2, (1980)

Galloway, R.L., *A history of coal mining in Great Britain* (London, 1969)

Greasley, D. 'Fifty Years of Coal Mining Productivity: The Record of the British Coal Industry before 1939' *The Journal of Economic History,* Vol. 50, No.4 (December. 1990)

Hair, P.E.H. Mortality from Violencein British Coal Mines, 1800-50, *Economic History Review,* Vol. 21 Issue 3 (December 1968) pp 545-561

Haldane. *Economic Geology of the Fife Coalfields area 1 Dunfermline and West Fife,* (Edinburgh, 1931)

Hazards magazine, issue. 116, (October-December 2011)

Heinrich, H.W. *Industrial Accident Prevention: A Scientific Approach,* (1930)

McGregor, M. *A Short History of the Scottish Coal Mining Industry* (1958)

McIntosh, C.B. 'Atmospheric Conditions and Explosions in Coal Mines' *Geographical Review,* Vol. 47, No.2 (April, 1957)

McIvor, A & Johnston, R., *Lethal Work: A History of the Asbestos Tragedy in Scotland,* (East Linton, 2000)

McIvor, A. & Johnston, R. 'Dangerous Work Hard men and Broken Bodies: Masculinity in the Clyde side Heavy Industries c.1930-1970.' *Labour History Review,* Vol 69, No 2, 2 August 2004

McIvor, A & Johnston, R., *Miners' lungs: a history of dust disease in British coal mining* (Aldershot, 2007)

Mills, C. 'Does Familiarity Breed Contempt?' Age and Accident Frequency in Cornish Non-Ferrous Metal Mining, 1881-1901' *British Mining,* No. 75 (2004)

Mills, C. *Regulating Health and Safety in the British Mining Industries, 1800-1914* (Surry, 2010)

Pike River, A failure to Learn, Produced by the Mines institute of Australia, PYT limited (2014)

Scottish Mining Website, 'Colliery Rules' (2005), <http://www.scottishmining.co.uk/13.html> [Accessed 24.10.2014]

Sinclair, J. *Coal Mining Law,* (London, 1958)

Taylor, T.J. *RC Accidents*, (London, 1854) p 1094 & Brown, G.I, The big Bang A history of explosives, (Stroud, 1998)

The Mining Association of Great Britain, *The Historical Review of Coal Mining,* (London, 1924)

World Coal Mining Organisation, <http://www.worldcol.org/coal-society/safety-issues/ >[Accessed 17/02/2015]

Wyman, M. *Hard Rock Epic: Western Miners and the Industrial Revolution, 1860-1910*, (California, 1992)

Zhao, Jian & Zhu, Weishen. *Stability Analysis and Modelling of Underground Excavations in Fractured Rocks.* (2003)

yes
I want morebooks!

Buy your books fast and straightforward online - at one of the world's fastest growing online book stores! Environmentally sound due to Print-on-Demand technologies.

Buy your books online at
www.get-morebooks.com

Kaufen Sie Ihre Bücher schnell und unkompliziert online – auf einer der am schnellsten wachsenden Buchhandelsplattformen weltweit!
Dank Print-On-Demand umwelt- und ressourcenschonend produziert.

Bücher schneller online kaufen
www.morebooks.de

OmniScriptum Marketing DEU GmbH
Heinrich-Böcking-Str. 6-8
D - 66121 Saarbrücken
Telefax: +49 681 93 81 567-9

info@omniscriptum.com
www.omniscriptum.com

Printed in Great Britain
by Amazon